CELEBRATING THE FAMILY NAME OF SULLIVAN

Celebrating the Family Name of Sullivan

Walter the Educator

Silent King Books
a WhichHead Entertainment Imprint

Copyright © 2024 by Walter the Educator

All rights reserved. No part of this book may be reproduced in any manner whatsoever without written permission except in the case of brief quotations embodied in critical articles and reviews.

First Printing, 2024

Disclaimer

This book is a literary work; the story is not about specific persons, locations, situations, and/or circumstances unless mentioned in a historical context. Any resemblance to real persons, locations, situations, and/or circumstances is coincidental. This book is for entertainment and informational purposes only. The author and publisher offer this information without warranties expressed or implied. No matter the grounds, neither the author nor the publisher will be accountable for any losses, injuries, or other damages caused by the reader's use of this book. The use of this book acknowledges an understanding and acceptance of this disclaimer.

Celebrating the Family Name of Sullivan is a memory book that belongs to the Celebrating Family Name Book Series by Walter the Educator. Collect them all and more books at WaltertheEducator.com

USE THE EXTRA SPACE TO DOCUMENT YOUR FAMILY MEMORIES THROUGHOUT THE YEARS

SULLIVAN

In emerald hills where whispers play,

Celebrating the Family Name of

Sullivan

And morning greets the rising day,

The name of Sullivan was born,

Amidst the dew of ancient morn.

Through misty vales and rugged lands,

Where ocean meets the shifting sands,

The Sullivan clan, with hearts so bold,

Wove tales of courage still untold.

With every breath of Gaelic air,

They walked with pride, their spirits fair,

For Sullivan means more than name—

It echoes like eternal flame.

From days of yore, in fields of green,

Where battles waged and kings had been,

The Sullivans stood firm and true,

With eyes that saw horizons new.

Celebrating the Family Name of

Sullivan

Their roots run deep in Ireland's soil,

Through centuries of sweat and toil,

Yet always, in each heart was found

A love for kin, for sacred ground.

Through storm and sun, through feast and strife,

The Sullivans embraced their life,

With laughter bright and spirits high,

They faced each challenge, reaching sky.

Oh, Sullivan, your name does ring,

Like wind that sweeps on eagle's wing,

Through every age, through time's long span,

The strength endures of Sullivan.

They built with hands both wise and skilled,

And dreamed with hearts forever filled,

With hope for futures bright and wide,

Celebrating the Family Name of

Sullivan

A journey taken side by side.

No mountain high, no sea too vast,

Could dim the spirit that would last,

For Sullivan blood runs bold and free,

A river flowing endlessly.

In homes where fires warm the night,

Their stories passed in soft moonlight,

Of ancestors who dared to rise,

And sought their fortune 'neath the skies.

ABOUT THE CREATOR

Walter the Educator is one of the pseudonyms for Walter Anderson. Formally educated in Chemistry, Business, and Education, he is an educator, an author, a diverse entrepreneur, and he is the son of a disabled war veteran. "Walter the Educator" shares his time between educating and creating. He holds interests and owns several creative projects that entertain, enlighten, enhance, and educate, hoping to inspire and motivate you. Follow, find new works, and stay up to date with Walter the Educator™

at WaltertheEducator.com

www.ingramcontent.com/pod-product-compliance
Lightning Source LLC
LaVergne TN
LVHW012052070526
838201LV00082B/3923